G000065960

A Plan for Joy in the Home

A Workbook on Organizing Your Day for Homeschooling Mothers

By Laura Dominick

Illustrated by Shaylynn Rackers

Published by Catholic Homeschooling Resources
www.catholic-homeschooling-resources.com
www.aplanforjoyinthehome.com

Acknowledgments

First off, I need to praise God for the idea for this book and the Holy Spirit for inspiring the words and ideas. God is good, all the time!

I would like to thank my husband for encouraging me and my children for putting up with all of the schedules I have tried on them over the years. Without all of them, I would have had little reason to be so organized.

Thank you to Andrew Schmiedicke for editing the first edition of this book and Jansina Grossman of Rivershore Books for doing the edit and layout for this second edition.

Thank you to Shaylynn Rackers who did all of the artwork. She was talented six years ago and is even more incredible now.

A huge thank you to all of my fellow homeschooling moms who participated in the initial workshops and then helped me to turn this into a book.

First edition copyright © 2011 Laura M Dominick
Second edition copyright © 2017 Laura M Dominick
978-0-615-63185-1
A Plan for Joy in the Home is under copyright. All rights reserved. With the exception of the forms and charts, which may be photocopied for immediate family members only, no part of this book may be reproduced in any form by any means—electronic, mechanical, or graphic—without prior written permission.

Table of Contents

Chapter One
Getting Started

*L*aundry and dishes and toys, oh my . . . breakfast and lunch and dinner, oh my . . . reading and history and math, oh my . . . babies and toddlers and teenagers, oh my! It's okay. Don't worry. Just close your eyes and repeat after me, "There's no place like home. There's no place like home."

And there isn't, is there? Despite all of the chaos, noise, and mess, there really isn't any place like home. Home with your family . . . all day, every day . . . day in and day out . . . Sorry, there I go again. Really, it doesn't have to be that bad. I might not have a pair of ruby slippers for you to put on and click together, but I have what I hope will bring order and joy into your home. Now, it will take some work on your part, and it won't happen overnight, but if you follow the plan, it *will* happen!

You might be wondering why I have named this "A Plan for Joy in the Home." Joy is the first tribute that we owe to God as a way of thanking Him for all that He has given us and done for us. God is pleased when He sees us full of joy and true gladness. Joy is a good example of charity to those around us—the first Christians were

Chapter One
Getting Started

such wonderful examples to the pagans around them mainly because of the joy with which they fulfilled their everyday duties. According to Francis Fernandez, author of *In Conversation with God*, "God wants the home where we live to be a bright and cheerful home, never a dark unhappy place full of tension." [1]

Do you feel that your home is a bright and cheerful home? Do you feel that you have a handle on your day-to-day activities to the point that you can radiate joy and show charity to those around you? If you don't have that joy, if you're not even sure of the last time you felt that joy, then it is my hope that once you finish this book and work through all of the exercises, you will have the tools you need to gain some control over your daily life so that you can devote more of your energy to being joyful. Mr. Fernandez goes on to say that having an

> ". . . interior joy is also the state of mind necessary for perfectly com-
> plying with our obligations. The greater our responsibility, the greater
> also our obligation to have this peace and joy to give to others, and the
> greater the urgency of recovering it when its habitual possession has
> been interrupted or disturbed." [2]

I am pretty sure that you have other things going on in your life that are robbing you of your joy, not just the fact that your life is disorganized. This is why it is so important to make a plan to build up your prayer life, as well as automate many of your day-to-day activities, so that you can focus on the really important things—so that you can focus on recovering that joy when it has been interrupted or disturbed.

Hopefully, by having a plan for your day, you will also find more time to do the things you want to do. People have asked me how I have time to keep up with my house, homeschool my kids, and still do all the other things that I do. I really think it comes down to the fact that I have streamlined many of my regular daily tasks. A lot of the things that go on in our house on a daily basis pretty much run on autopilot. Everyone knows what to do and when to do it (although that doesn't mean they don't have to be reminded often!). We don't have to spend a lot of time deciding what needs to be done and who is going to get it done. If you are faithful to working through this plan, then you should be able to say the same thing of your own life.

Many of you have heard the story of the professor who showed a glass jar filled with rocks to his class and asked the class if the jar was full. When they said yes, he poured in some pea-gravel and then asked them if it was full. When they said yes, he poured in some sand and then asked them if it was full. When they said yes, he poured in some water. Finally, the jar really was full. What does this mean for us? As Elizabeth Yank pointed out in a talk she gave on homeschooling, it *does not* mean that we should continue to shove more things into a day that already looks full. What she said it means is that if we didn't put the big rocks into the jar first, we would have never been able to add them later. We have to work our way from the big things to the smaller things.

So what are the big rocks in your life? What are the things that must happen each day in order for your family to function properly? If you leave these "big rocks" out, chances are you will find that you keep getting frustrated with the way things are going. Each of us has different rocks in our lives. It is impossible for me to cover every one of them for every person, so this book will focus on some universal big rocks: prayer time, chore time, school time, meal time, and personal/husband/family time. We will take a look at each of these areas and then spend some time praying about how these big rocks fit into the jar of our day. It is after you fit these rocks into your jar that you can then begin to add the smaller rocks, sand, and water. This should give you a good idea of just how much "free" time you have in your day to take on other things without going crazy.

In many Christian books you read or talks you hear on organization, inevitably the author will bring up Martha and Mary. This book won't disappoint you. I know that Martha and Mary were both very holy women and devoted to Christ and their faith, so I am not trying to show one in a better light than the other, but, beginning with Martha, let's just imagine how each of them would be as homeschooling mothers.

Let's envision Martha rising promptly with her daily agenda already spinning in her head. She would begin her day with prayer and would carry the presence of God with her throughout her day. Breakfast would be made and the kitchen would be tidied. The kids would be up on time, dressed, and ready to begin their day of school—teeth and hair brushed, rooms neat, beds made, pencils sharpened. School would go like clockwork while the laundry was getting done and the toddlers were happily occupied. A sense of joy and peace would permeate the household. Another virtue that would also be noticeable would be orderliness. While there might be a slight mess here or there, the entire house would radiate a sense of organization. School would be finished; the kids would have their free time while Martha would catch up on some correspondence. Dinner would be readied and the kids and house would be tidied before Dad came home. The evening would be spent as a family, having fun and praying together.

Mary's home would also be one of peace and joy, although maybe slightly less organized. She would also rise promptly and begin her day in prayer. Maybe her prayer time might go a little longer every once in a while and throw off her schedule, but she wouldn't mind. She, too, would get breakfast ready and the kids up and ready for school. Again, her home would be neat, but maybe there might be a few more messes around. I envision Mary as the type of mother who would be willing to throw off the whole schedule just because a bird decided to build a nest outside her window. She might spend the whole morning with her children watching the bird and reveling in the marvels of God's creation. Dinner may or may not be precisely on time, but it would be cooked with care nonetheless. Their evening would also be spent as a family having fun and praying together, but I imagine their house having a bit slower, calmer pace to it.

Now, in both scenarios there is a lot of good. Martha is a prayerful woman and she has many virtues, as does Mary. However, our Lord reprimanded Martha for being caught up in her to do list. On the other hand, as much as we might want to always be like Mary, don't you find that sometimes it is impossible because there is something that just has to be done? I think that, because of the society we live in, we will be peaceful and joyful homeschooling mothers if we take the best of Martha and Mary and build our day with that in mind. Let us be an organized doer like Martha, but like Mary let us also be able to stop and smell the roses and delight in the day that the Lord has given us. Like both women, it is crucial that we begin and end our day with the Lord, as well as strive to always keep Him a part of our entire day.

So what is stopping you? Is it that you just don't know how to get started? Are you organizationally challenged? Are you a "quick-start" personality — someone who gets enthusiastic about some new idea but just can't follow through? Do you get mired down in details and lose the big picture? Are you upset because you've been down this road before but haven't gotten very far? Don't get frustrated. Read this quote from the book *In Conversation with God*. Francis Fernandez, commenting on how the disciples react when they realize that they only have 5 loaves and 2 fishes to feed the multitudes, states,

"The disciples see objective reality. They know that this small amount of food will not suffice to feed the multitude. This is what may happen to us when we take stock of our own strengths and possibilities. The difficulties before us may appear larger than life and beyond our power to influence. Mere human objectivity can lead us to discouragement and pessimism. It can cause us to forget the radical optimism which is part and parcel of the Christian vocation. As popular wisdom would have it: He who fails to include God in his reckonings does not know how to add. He does not know how to add because he leaves out the most important factor (which is, of course, God Himself) . . . Christian optimism is rooted in God, who says to us: I am with you always, to the end of time. With Him we can do anything . . . Cast away that despair produced by the realization of your weakness. It's true: financially you are a zero, and socially another zero, and another in virtues, and another in talents . . . But to the left of these zeros is Christ. And what an immeasurable figure it turns out to be. How this realization changes our entire outlook at the hour of beginning an apostolic work, at the moment of personal conversion, in the realities of ordinary life!"[3]

Don't get discouraged if you have tried before to be organized and have "failed." Accept it, go over what went wrong, change what you can, pick up your pencil and try again, realizing that Christ is right beside you to help you along the way.

The author continues,

"A Christian's optimism gets strong reinforcement from prayer. Christian optimism is not a sugary optimism; nor is it a mere human coincidence that everything will turn out all right. It is an optimism that sinks its roots in an awareness of our freedom, and in the sure knowledge of the power of grace. It is an optimism which leads us to make demands on ourselves, to struggle to respond at every moment to God's call."[4]

There are a few key points in this last paragraph that we need to focus on. First: Christian optimism gets strong reinforcement from prayer. This explains why we will be spending a lot of time on the prayer time section. Second: It is an optimism which leads us to make demands on ourselves. Remember this when you get discouraged or are feeling lazy. Being organized is hard work. It requires you to always be on top of things; it takes a lot of time! But it is worth it. It is what we are all called to be. We were created in the image and likeness of God. Therefore, we have to realize that we are being called to imitate Him in His orderliness.

Consider this a call from God. This is a new start for you: a more prayerful, more organized, more peaceful, and more joyful you. Don't forget that you are never alone in this struggle. You have the Body of Christ and the Communion of Saints. We are all in this together—praying and suffering for one another. We also know that the Lord is just waiting for us to give Him our meager five loaves and two fishes so that He can multiply them in amazing ways.

As you read through this book, you will notice that there are various prayers interspersed throughout each section. When you reach these points, pause for a moment and really pray the prayer so that the time you spend on each section will be inspired and fruitful. It might also be helpful for you to read through the entire book first and then go back and read it again, this time taking the time to do all of the workbook pages. Sometimes getting the overall picture helps with the individual parts.

So, right now, pause for a moment and pray the following prayer:

> *"Teach me, dear Lord, to appreciate the value of time. Let me not think it is a small matter to waste time in idle reading or conversation. Help me see that time is the talent You have entrusted to our keeping, to be used for the greater profit of souls. It is not ours but Yours. While we are wasting time the enemy is alert and working for the downfall of the human race. On the day of judgment You will demand a strict account of every idle word we have spoken, and reward us according to the use we made of this precious gift of Your bounty."[5] Amen.*

Chapter Two
Prayer Time

*I*f we are lucky, it happens to us every day: We wake up! But how do we wake up? In a panic? Already behind for the day? Does it take us 30 minutes to wake up or do we pop out of bed? Let's begin our discussion about prayer with the simple act of waking up because this one moment can set the tone for the whole day. St. Jose Marie Escriva calls this the moment when we first wake up the "heroic moment." By rolling over and going back to sleep we can make it a moment of defeat, or by getting up promptly we can turn it into the first prayer of the day.

An important part of your plan will be for you to pick a consistent time to wake up. Do whatever you have to do to get up: set an alarm (or two); have someone else wake you; plead with your Guardian Angel. Do whatever it takes! At the appointed time, you are going to open your eyes and say "Serviam," which means "I will serve You, Lord"—thus consecrating your day to the Lord.

Most of you already know that prayer is a crucial part of your day. You know that the more you pray, the better things go—not saying that everything will be perfect, but that you will be better able to handle whatever happens to come your way because you have invited the Lord into your day. You also know that when your prayer routine goes by the wayside, so does your sanity. Little by little you notice things getting out of control, ending up in chaos more often than not. It might take you a while to realize that it is because little by little you have let your prayer time be taken over by more pressing matters. The time you set aside in your schedule for prayer is going to have to become set in concrete. You will have to guard this time like a precious jewel. If you do not have that attitude about your prayer time, then it will begin to slip ever so slowly from your grasp.

You have to realize and internalize the fact that if you do not spend time every day in prayer, you are not going to be able to get out there and fulfill the apostolate that God wants you to fulfill. This apostolate might be just within your home or it might include something within your church or your community. Whatever it is, if you do not fill up your tank with grace and peace, you will have nothing to give to anyone else. You must also realize that your prayer needs are probably going to be different from other people. It might take daily Mass and three rosaries for you to maintain your cool, while it may take someone else only one rosary. Finally, understand that your prayer needs will probably change from time to time. That's okay. Set your plan, but be willing to change it when necessary. It is always a good thing to revise your prayer plan about once or twice a year to keep up with any changes in your routine.

So what is a good prayer plan? Let's take some time right now to look at what other people see as a minimum daily requirement for prayer:

Father Pablo Straub, in a talk he gave on the Holy Family, said that the *minimum* prayers for every day consist of: the blessing of the food (and not just at dinner), the Angelus at least once a day, daily Mass, the Chaplet of Divine Mercy, and the Rosary. When discussing daily Mass, Father made a point of saying that many people think that getting to daily Mass is impossible. For some it truly is, but for others, there are obstacles that appear to be standing in the way that would be relatively easy to do away with. He states that some people think that getting to Mass takes up too much of their time. To the world it might appear that we are wasting time by getting to Mass every day. In Father's eyes, however, he feels that "the best way to make time is to waste time." Waste time in daily prayer, waste time in getting to Mass. **Be faithful** to this and you will be amazed at how much time you really do have in a day.

The Miles Christi priests, while preaching the Spiritual Exercises of St. Ignatius, talk about the importance of spending 15 minutes a day in silent meditation, 30 minutes a day slowly reading a good spiritual book, daily Mass, Rosary, and ending the day with a particular and general examination of conscience.

We all know that it is important for us to give to God the first fruits of all that we have. Since He has given us 24 hours, wouldn't it be good for us to give back to Him 10% of those 24 hours? Doing the math, that would mean that we should rightfully give to God 2.4 hours or 2 hours and 24 minutes of each day. That seems like it is impossible to do, but let's take a look at it more closely:

Morning meditation and prayers 30 minutes
Daily Mass 30 minutes
Family Rosary 30 minutes

Only three things and you're already at 1½ hours. Throw in some mid-day prayers, spiritual reading time, and offering of a time of work or suffering to the Lord and you can easily get to 2.4 hours. Of course, don't let this scare you so that you don't do anything; and don't get legalistic either, thinking that you have failed because you've gone four days only spending 1 hour in prayer instead of 2.4 hours. Let's just use this as a guideline and see how generous we can be with our time. Remember, God is never outdone in His generosity. It is true that the more time you give to Him, the more time you will find to do the things you need to do.

It's time right now to get practical! We're about to get started working on the prayer time worksheet. This book is organized in such a way that if you do all of the worksheets as they are presented, filling in your main schedule at the end will be very easy to do. Each of the areas that we will cover has its own worksheets so that you can spend some time thinking about and organizing each of them independently. The final exercise is to put all of your work together into a main schedule that will help organize your day. All that being said, let's take a moment right now to pray the following prayer before we get started:

Lord Jesus, help me to rise promptly with the alarm in the morning. I know from experience how much this first act of sacrifice can affect my meditation and consequently my whole day. Let me offer You the self-conquest it requires as atonement for my past self-indulgence and a petition for the strength of character which You look for in Your devoted servants. (Father John Hardon)

Lord, help me to plan the day of prayer that You would like me to have. Let me be generous in devoting time to You in prayer, but save me from making my prayer life so complicated that I can't keep up with it. Guide me and give me Your wisdom, Lord. Amen.

On the next page you will notice that there is a prayer time worksheet that is already filled out. This is included to help you get started. At the top of the page are some prayers that you might wish to consider incorporating into your day. The finished sheet shows the prayers that I will pray throughout the day, an estimate of how much time I will need, when I will pray them, and who will participate. Take some time to look the sample page over and then spend some time organizing your prayer time on the blank worksheet that follows. You might want to photocopy each of the blank worksheets so you'll always have the original to work with at a later date.

One more thing before you begin. You might be thinking that you already have an organized prayer life, or if it isn't organized, at least it is a prayer life that is working well for you. If that is the case *do not* feel that you have to change it. Simply fill in what you are doing now so that you can reference the information later. Again, you do not have to change something that is already working for you. The point is not for you to do everything the way I suggest. I am throwing out ideas in case you are frustrated with the way your current system isn't working!

Sample Prayer Time Worksheet

Some suggestions of prayers to incorporate into your day

Daily Mass
Serviam prayer
Morning Offering
15 minutes of meditation
Prayers to Jesus, Mary, and Joseph
Guardian Angel prayer
Memorare
Rosary
Chaplet of Divine Mercy
The Angelus

Meal prayers
Night prayers
General examination
Particular examination
Prayers to a favorite saint
Litanies
Scripture Reading
Novenas
Consecration prayers
Adoration of the Blessed Sacrament

Prayer	How much time?	Morn/Noon /Night	Who will participate?
Meditation	15 minutes	Morning	Me
Personal Morning prayers	20 minutes	Morning	Me
Scripture reading	5 minutes	Morning	Me
Daily Mass	30 minutes	Morning	All
Lunch prayers	5 minutes	Noon	All
Mid-day prayers	10 minutes	Noon	Me
Spiritual reading	15 minutes	Noon	Me
Meal prayers	5 minutes	Night	All
Rosary	30 minutes	Night	All
Examination	10 minutes	Night	Me
Night prayers	10 minutes	Night	Me

Prayer Time Worksheet

Some suggestions of prayers to incorporate into your day

Daily Mass	Meal prayers
Serviam prayer	Night prayers
Morning Offering	General examination
15 minutes of meditation	Particular examination
Prayers to Jesus, Mary, and Joseph	Prayers to a favorite saint
Guardian Angel prayer	Litanies
Memorare	Scripture Reading
Rosary	Novenas
Chaplet of Divine Mercy	Consecration prayers
The Angelus	Adoration of the Blessed Sacrament

Prayer	How much time?	Morn/Noon/Night	Who will participate?

After you've spent some time on this and filled in your chart, you should have a good idea of what you'd like your prayer life to look like. Remember, of course, that not every day will be perfect, but at least you have a plan to guide you. Sometimes just having something written down that you can follow is enough to keep you accountable so that your prayer routine can become a habit.

You can set this sheet aside for now and clear your mind; you are ready to move on to the next chapter!

Chapter Three
Chore Time

Now that we have tackled what I feel is the most important part of everyone's day, we can move on to something easier . . . chores. As homeschooling mothers, we can oftentimes feel overwhelmed with the amount of things we need to do each day. If we expend all of our energy on schooling, then the house falls apart. If we expend all of our energy on the house, then our kids fall apart. The key to solving this problem is balance.

Let's ask ourselves a few questions. What must my house look like each day in order for me to maintain my sanity? Must the bathrooms be shining every day and the house spotless or can neat suffice? What does my *husband* say the house should look like every day? Does he just want a clear path to the dinner table or is he expecting the children and house to shine? Is there any flexibility in either of these viewpoints? Can you both come to terms about what is doable and acceptable? Keep this in mind as we progress through this section.

We've all heard the phrase "Cleanliness is next to Godliness." Let me point out that it does not say "Obsessive cleanliness is next to Godliness." If there is a string on the floor that was just vacuumed a few minutes ago, picking it up and mumbling under your breath about how nothing ever stays clean around here is not going to bring you closer to God. I don't think that God is grading us on whether we have a wrinkle in our sheet or a stain on our counter. I think what He is paying attention to is whether or not we are trying to keep our home neat and orderly, even if we have to begin again each day with a new resolve.

On the other hand, however, I think we must ask ourselves whether or not our house meets what would be considered minimal standards of cleanliness. I'm not talking about not having a pile here or there in every room. I'm talking about whether or not you would mind if someone popped over because they needed a glass of water and a chance to put their feet up. Would you be able to find a clean glass? Would you be able to find the couch?

I think a good rule of thumb regarding the state of our house is that it should be within 1 hour of being ready to be seen by outsiders without feeling embarrassed (let's say ½ hour if you have some able-bodied children). If someone were to call you and ask if they could stop over for a visit in an hour, could you get your house picked up and looking presentable within that timeframe? If not, you need to begin thinking about what your problem areas are. There's a big difference between a house with toys strewn around the family room and a house where you can barely find an open space. Again, I don't think that God is looking for perfection in this area, just a good amount of effort to do your best.

"But I have so much stuff, I don't even have a place for it all," you might be thinking. De-junking your home is a whole other issue. De-junking needs to be done. It takes a lot of time as well as mental and emotional energy. If, however, you are going to keep your home looking presentable and enjoyable to live in, you need to make sure that there is a place for everything (and not in a pile under your bed, in your closet, or on top of your dresser). I am going to suggest that you not worry right now about all of the clutter and about how you are ever going to de-junk. Right now I want you to focus on getting control of your day so that you can find the time to tackle such a project. Once you have a plan of action for your day, tackling big projects like that will be much easier.

Let's start focusing on that day-to-day stuff. What you need to do right now is to think about the things that need to get done every day in order for your home to run smoothly. One big factor in deciding how many of these daily tasks you can undertake and how much time you can devote to them is taking into account the number and ages of your children.

If you have at least one child who can walk steadily on their own, then you have a child who can help with chores. The younger the child, the more enthusiastic they usually will be to help you. Catch them while they are young. If you put off training them to help you, it will be nothing but an uphill battle. My daughter Rebecca was the best 5-year-old vacuumer I have ever had. Mary, at age 5, could wash a sink full of non-glass dishes reasonably well. I will be the first to admit that it amazes me how much they can do at such a young age. I also know that my older three girls, while they are very helpful and obedient, are not as industrious and don't have as much of a "roll your sleeves up and get the job done" attitude as the younger four because I waited too long to have them help me with the chores. I always took the "I can do it faster myself" approach with them and I can now see how that had a negative impact on their wanting to help out.

As we go through the next section about what needs to get done, when it needs to get done, and who is going to do it, try to come up with chores that each child can do. Obviously you know your own children better than I do, but don't cut them short. Give them a chance to show you how good of a worker they can be. Challenge them. Give them incentives. Discipline them if you have to, but get them involved in helping to keep the house running smoothly. It is a win-win-win situation: Your house is neat and you are more at ease; your children learn the value of hard work (and the negative consequences for not doing it); and your husband comes home to a neat house in which he can relax.

Before we move on to the work part of this chapter, let us stop and say a prayer:

Dear Lord, help me to see the value in having a neat and orderly home. Help me to use prudence in planning the daily tasks that need to be done—not leaving important things out, but not overloading everyone with chores so that there is a rebellion. Give me the virtue of perseverance because I know that keeping my house clean takes time and energy. Help me to set good goals for my family and then give me the grace to stick with them. Amen.

The first thing you should do is break down into categories the chores that you think need to be done in your home on a daily basis, a weekly basis, a monthly basis and every once in a while. We are going to focus on planning out the daily chores, but it is very helpful to have a list of things that need to be done at other times. This way, you can assign people to each of those other chores as well as assign when they are to be done. For example—who cleans the bathroom every week, who dusts the ceiling fans every month, and who will help wash windows over summer break.

On the next page, you'll see that I've included a sample list of chores to help you organize your thoughts. Use this list to jog your memory about what needs to be done in your house. The chart following that is a sample chart that has some of those chores filled in under the frequency with which they will be done. Take some time right now to look at this sample list and then fill out the first chore worksheet.

Sample List of Chores

Kitchen	Living Room/Family Room
Wash dishes	Dust furniture
Dry dishes, put away	Vacuum carpets/sweep floors
Fill dishwasher	Clean fireplace
Empty dishwasher	Dust wall hangings/pictures
Clean sink	Wash drapes/blinds
Sweep floor	Clean mirrors
Wash floor	Vacuum lamp shades/furniture
Shake/vacuum rug	Move furniture to clean underneath
Wipe stovetop	Remove cobwebs
Clean oven	Dust ceiling fan/light fixtures
Wipe down entire stove	**Meal Related**
Clean microwave in/out	Prepare meals
Defrost freezer	Put away food
Clean out fridge of old food	Set table
Wash inside of fridge	Clear table
Clean out cabinets	Bake
Wipe down cabinet doors	**Miscellaneous**
Clean out drawers	Water plants
Wipe off counters	Clean fingerprints from the walls
Wipe down small appliances	Straighten misc. closets
Empty garbage	Straighten shoes
Clean light fixtures	Straighten jackets
Clean ceiling fan	Get mail
Wipe down walls	Wash windows and screens
Bathroom	**Pet Related**
Clean tub/shower	Walk the dog
Clean sinks	Clean up the yard
Clean toilets	Clean the litter box
Wash shower door/curtain	Feed and water the pets
Wash/vacuum rugs	Clean any cages
clean mirrors	**Laundry**
Clean out medicine cabinet	Sort laundry
Wipe down walls	Wash laundry
Sweep floor	Dry laundry
Wash floor	Fold clothes
Clean out cabinets/drawers	Distribute clean clothing
Bedrooms	Iron clothing
Make beds	**Bedrooms (Cont.)**
Change sheets	Wash blind/curtains
Clean under beds	Hang up/put away clothes
Vacuum rug	Dust ceiling fan/light fixtures
Dust furniture	**Other**
Clean closet/drawers	

Sample Chore Time Worksheet 1

Daily	Monthly
Dishes—wash, dry, put away for all meals	Dust furniture in rooms
Sweep floors	Dust ceiling fans
Pick up assigned rooms	Change bed sheets
Take out garbage	
Laundry	
Make beds and straighten rooms	
Put away clothes	
Meal preparation	
Animal chores	
Wipe table/counters for each meal	
Put away food from meals	

Weekly	Once in a while
Clean bathrooms	Wash windows
Wash floors	Wash screens
Vacuum rugs	Clean carpets
Shop for groceries	Wash out fridge
Go through fridge	Dust-mop corners and air vents
	Defrost freezer

Chore Time Worksheet 1

Daily	Monthly

Weekly	Once in a while

Now that you have your lists, let's take a closer look at that daily list of chores. On the next page, you will see a chart similar to the one we used for our prayer time. What you will do is take each daily chore and decide roughly how long it will take, what time of the day it will be done, and who will do it. For right now, just assign each chore to a general timeframe. When we get to putting them on the master schedule, you will notice that some chores can be grouped together into one ½ hour time block, such as: get breakfast ready, eat, clear spot, and put away food. Another example would be lunchtime where you could do all of your lunch-related chores in a one-hour time break. Don't worry that you will have to find individual slots on your schedule for each chore you put down. This is just a tool to help you organize all of the things you want to have done every day and who it is who will do them.

Just a reminder: I highly encourage you to work on each worksheet as it comes up in the workbook. If you don't do them in order, chances are you just won't do them and then when it comes time to put it together into one master schedule, you'll be missing pieces.

Sample Chore Time Worksheet 2

Chore	How Much Time?	Morn /Noon /Night	Who Will Do It?
Get breakfast ready	15 minutes	morning	me
clear breakfast dishes	5 minutes	morning	all
put away breakfast food	5 minutes	morning	Timmy
wash dishes	15 minutes	morning	me
make beds, dress, brush, straighten rooms	15 minutes	morning	all
laundry	10 minutes	morn/aft	Teresa
empty dish drainer/washer	5 minutes	aft	Megan
get lunch ready	15 minutes	aft	me
clear lunch dishes	5 minutes	aft	all
wash dishes	15 minutes	aft	Anthony
put away lunch food	5 minutes	aft	Timmy
sweep kitchen floor	5 minutes	aft	Amanda
pick up assigned rooms	20 minutes	aft	all
take out garbage	5 minutes	aft	Timmy
feed animals	15 minutes	aft	Amanda and one other
prepare dinner	1 hour	eve	me, Amanda, or Megan
set table	5 minutes	eve	Mary
empty dish drainer/washer	5 minutes	eve	Megan
clear and wipe table/counters	15 minutes	eve	Anthony
wash dishes	25 minutes	eve	Teresa
dry and put away dishes	25 minutes	eve	Rebecca
sweep kitchen and dining room	10 minutes	eve	Amanda
ready for bed, put clothes away	10 minutes	eve	all

Chore Time Worksheet 2

Chore	How Much Time?	Morn/Noon /Night	Who Will Do It?

Chapter Four
School Time

S ince we've been talking about our children learning things, we might as well move on to . . . school time. This section is probably the key reason why we need to have a schedule in the first place. I'll tell you right now, this is the hardest section to get down on paper and stick with. The main reason for the difficulty is that every day seems to be different. How do we handle all of those differences? It will help if you look at your schedule as the backbone of your day. It is your guide to turn back to if you get lost in confusion. It is basically there to keep you on track so that if you get thrown off course for a few hours, you can look to your watch to see what time it is and then look to your schedule to see what you should be doing, and then go do it.

Since the school day takes up a major portion of our day, I think that now is a good time to make a few important points about schedules in general:

I think it is best that you do not make a schedule for each day of the week. If you do that, you will then need to make a schedule to keep track of your schedules. You will, in short, drive yourself crazy. If our days are really all that different and a different schedule for each day is the only way that things will work, then give it a shot. My advice is to try to work with the least amount of daily schedules as possible.

You will *not* become a slave to your schedule. Do not obsess if it is 10:35 and you are supposed to be doing geography but your kids are still engrossed in their spelling words. Do your best to finish up one subject and then move them on to the next. If you really want to stick to the timeframes you set up, give them a 5-minute warning before it is time to switch subjects. After a while, my children knew exactly what time the next subject started and they were usually the ones calling me!

On the flip-side, don't spend the time to make a schedule and then disregard it every day. If you find that it is impossible to stick to what you had planned, then something is wrong. Go back over your schedule and rework it so that it is doable. Whatever you do, don't say after only one week, "See, it doesn't work. I will never be able to be organized." Rework your plan and try again. Maybe the problem is that you are trying to cover too much in too little time. Either devote more time in your day to schoolwork or redo your schoolwork to fit in the time you have set aside during the day.

Important note: If your children need you to help them with their work or at least need you there so that they can ask you questions, then *don't* schedule yourself to be doing something else. If it is school time and you are needed, then make sure that you are there! This may seem logical, but given that there is so much in any given day for us mothers to do, it is easy to find ourselves engrossed in something else right when our kids need help or direction. It is then easy for us to get irritated with them for interrupting us when, in reality, we should have been more available to them.

If you have only a few children that you are schooling, then your scheduling shouldn't be that difficult. If you have a lot of children to school, then it gets more complicated to spread yourself around. Let's face it: no matter how many children you have, you still can only be in one place at a time. I think that the reason God does not allow us to bilocate is because then we would not be giving our undivided attention to the task or person at hand. The ability to multi-task might come in handy at times, but it really does prevent us from living fully in the present moment. If we are trying to do more than one thing at a time, are we really giving our full attention to either of them? Are we living the sacrament of the present moment by trying to do two things at once? You might be able to accomplish them, but is that really living that present moment to the fullest?

Okay, I'll get off my soapbox and get back to my previous thought. The more children you are trying to school, the more time it is going to take you if you want/need to sit with each child for each subject. Remember, the time has to come from somewhere. If you are going to be able to stay sane, you will need to decide what constitutes the rocks in your life and find a way to place them so that they all fit. If individually teaching each of your five children every subject is what is important to you, then you will have to realize that this will take a big chunk of your day and you will need to take time away from other areas of your life (with the exception of your prayer life!!).

There are other options, however, for ways to teach your children. If you find that you are struggling to get all your schoolwork in every day and you just can't imagine devoting any more time to it, then maybe you need to rethink how you teach your children. Consider these options:

- Letting your children do more work on their own
- Limiting the number of subjects they have to do in one day
- Teaching two children close in age some of the same subjects
- Doing some subjects only a few days a week instead of every day
- Finding two or four subjects that could be accomplished in a semester or quarter and then covering them in that timeframe instead of scheduling them all over the whole year
- Considering unit studies so that you can teach groups of children at the same time
- Looking into a more student-directed way of learning, like the Founding Fathers of our country learned

Again, this topic is a seminar in and of itself. I can only touch on some ideas for you to think about.

A few more points before we start to work on your school schedule:

- Remember, we have not put this all down into a main schedule yet, so you have to keep the big picture in the back of your mind. If you get so caught up in planning your school day that you forget to leave some time for prayers and chores, then you will have a big problem when you try to put it all together.
- Have a general idea in your mind (one that you are willing to be flexible with) of what time school will begin and end. Generally speaking, I

have seen that a lot of families use the hours from 9:00–12:00 and 1:00–3:00 for school. This leaves time for things before school, an hour break for lunch, chores and recess, and some time in the afternoon for your children and you to take care of other things.

• My oldest daughter's advice was to plan math as the first subject so that you are fresh when you do it and you get it out of the way!

• If you know that most days you are gone at a certain time of the day—like three mornings a week you have some kind of lesson in the morning, or you go to Mass at a different time every day—plan subjects during that time that you can take with you or that you might be able to double up on the next day. In other words, don't plan your history unit study for a time when you know that people are going to be missing or you are all going to be in the car.

• Remember not to schedule yourself or one of the other children to be in two places at the same time.

• If you have toddlers or babies that are causing you to become frustrated, try scheduling some time for each of the older kids to play with or entertain the younger ones for you. At the minimum, try to do this for those crucial subjects that you have to devote your whole attention to (like math with your 3rd grader).

• Lastly, I know many families who spend a portion of their school day doing apostolate work or other non-book work. If this is how your family works, then put your apostolate or other work in as part of your day. However, if you also have "book work" that you want your kids to do, make sure that it has a set section in your plan so that it gets done.

It's time to stop and pray before we go on!

> *Dear Lord, help me to remember as I begin to plan our school day that the most important lesson for me to teach my children is to know You, to love You, and to serve You. Help me to plan their subjects so that we can enjoy learning together. Again, give me Your wisdom so that I may challenge them in their studies but not overload them with unnecessary work. Holy Spirit, guide my hand as I plan this important part of our day. Amen.*

I have included a prayer written by Fr. Hardon for teachers that you can use during your school day if you would like.

A Teacher's Prayer *by Fr. John Hardon*

Dear Lord, help me teach my children how to live this life on earth, to face its struggles and improve their worth in the Church and in civil society. May the result of my message to them be not just a lesson in a book, but their choice of right from wrong. I ask Your guidance, Lord, to fill my place, to do my part in forging character and bringing Your grace to their hearts. Amen.

I know that I learn best by seeing what other people have done. Therefore, I have enclosed samples of the school time worksheets that you will be working on. Nobody else is going to have the same school set up as you do, but I know that it helps me to see an example of what I am supposed to be trying to figure out. Before you begin, take a look at all of the sample schedules.

You will now begin to form a rough sketch of what your school time is going to look like. Maybe what you are already doing is working well and you would like to keep it that way. If so, just fill it in on the worksheets. If you don't know how your day should be going or you are not happy with the way it has been going, now is the time to play around with it. At the bare minimum, choose a starting and ending time for your school day. Remember that you will need to allow time for prayers, chores, and meals. Don't worry right now about other things like lessons that pop up at odd times during the week. Unless they occur every day at the same time, we're not even going to put them on the worksheet.

One more reminder before I give you some handy steps for filling out the following section of worksheets. I have provided all of these worksheets to help you break things down to smaller levels because some people need to see things like that in order for them to make sense. If you are not that kind of person, then move right on over to the first worksheet that you can work with. In other words, if you don't need it, don't use it (and don't get stressed out about it being there and not using it!).

On Worksheet 1, list your children's names across the top. Then underneath their names, list all of the subjects they are either currently studying or will be studying this year.

Once you are done with that, go to Worksheet 2, where you will break those subjects down into two categories: subjects that they need you to teach and subjects they will teach to each other. This section might include older children spending reading time with younger children, maybe musical instrument teaching time, or even time that one child might be assigned to help with the baby or toddler.

The final worksheet will be the remaining subjects that they can do on their own. When you are done with this sheet, all the classes that you had listed on Worksheet 1 should be transferred over to a spot on either Worksheet 2 or 3. On Worksheet 3 you may want to draw a line between students and tally up the amount of time each student needs individually each day.

Sample School Time Worksheet 1

What are your school hours going to be?　　　*9:00–3:00*

Megan	Teresa	Rebecca	Timmy	Mary	Anthony	
Math	Math	Math	Math	Math	Math	
Biology	Religion	French	French	French	Phonics	
Website	Botany	History	History	History	Reading	
French	French	Religion	Typing	Religion	Handwrit-ing	
Am. Govt	World Hist	US Geog	US Geog	Hand-writing		
World hist	World Lit	Beau-tiful girlhood	Religion	Spelling		
Apolo-getics	Piano		Piano			

School Time Worksheet 1

What are your school hours going to be?

Notes:

Sample School Time Worksheet 2

Subjects I need to teach	To Whom	How much time do I need?
Math	Megan and Teresa	½ hour
Math	Timmy and Rebecca	½ hour
History/Govt Unit study	Timmy, Rebecca, Mary, and Anthony	1 hour
Letters, numbers and reading	Anthony	½ hour
Geography	Timmy and Rebecca	½ hour
Math	Mary and Anthony	½ hour

Subjects they teach to each other	Teacher/student	How much time?
Piano	Teresa/Timmy	½ hour
Reading stories	Rebecca/Mary	½ hour each
Play	Anthony/Mary	½ hour

School Time Worksheet 2

Subjects I need to teach	To Whom	How much time do I need?

Subjects they teach to each other	Teacher/student	How much time?

Sample School Time Worksheet 3

Subjects they do on their own	Student	How much time?
Biology	Megan	½ hour
Website	Megan	1 hour
French	Megan	½ hour
American Govt	Megan	½ hour
History	Megan	½ hour
Apologetics	Megan	½ hour
Religion	Teresa	½ hour
Botany	Teresa	½ hour
French	Teresa	½ hour
History	Teresa	½ hour
Literature	Teresa	½ hour
Piano	Teresa	½ hour
Web site	Teresa	1 hour
French	Rebecca	½ hour
Religion	Rebecca	½ hour
Beautiful Girlhood	Rebecca	½ hour
Grammar/Spelling	Rebecca	½ hour
Grammar/Spelling	Timmy	½ hour
French	Timmy	½ hour
Typing	Timmy	½ hour
Religion	Timmy	½ hour
Grammar	Mary	½ hour
Handwriting	Mary	½ hour
Spelling	Mary	½ hour
Handwriting	Anthony	½ hour

School Time Worksheet 3

Subjects they do on their own	Student	How much time?

Chapter Five
Meal Time

I don't know about you, but food consumes a large part of my time each day. I spend more of my day in my kitchen than any other room in my house. If I did not have a way to organize my meal times, my life would be far more chaotic than necessary. Because we have a large family, I have found it vital for maintaining my sanity to make meals more of a routine in our household. If you struggle with organizing your meals, hopefully this section will help you figure out how to bring them under control.

The first thing I had to do was to organize my grocery shopping and dinner meal planning. A number of years ago, I took a notebook with me to the grocery store and I wrote down all of the things that I normally would buy in the order in which they appeared in the aisles. I made this form up in Excel so that now I can just print about 10 copies at a time and keep them in the planning notebook that I keep on my desk. This way, throughout the week, I can flip to my grocery list and either circle or write in any items that we need. No more notes all over the desk that I then have to compile into a list later on. This system has worked very well for me for quite a long time. It might be only somewhat helpful if you shop at multiple stores or if you shop at a store that constantly moves its merchandise around. If that is the case, then hopefully you can live with your list not matching the order of the store.

In order to organize my dinners, I keep a blank calendar page for the week in a page protector that I hang on my refrigerator door. You can print your calendar page off of the computer, make one on a spreadsheet or just use one of the many calendars that you get in the mail each year. I try to do my grocery shopping on the same day every week—usually on Thursday. Each week before I go to the store, I take my calendar sheet off of the refrigerator and fill in the dinners for the upcoming week. I have tried filling in dinners for a whole month at a time, which makes shopping even easier, but it seems that lately I just can't seem to think that far in advance. After I have decided what dinners we will be having for the next week, I proceed to make sure that I have all of the necessary ingredients. Anything I don't have gets written on that week's list. After that, I just fill in the other necessities I will need for the week for breakfast, lunch, snacks, personal items, etc.

This system of planning out a week's worth of dinners is a lifesaver, especially when you don't live near a grocery store. No longer do I have to agonize over what to eat each night for dinner or wonder if I even have all of the ingredients I need. Every morning I look at the calendar to remind myself what we are having and I then take out the appropriate meat to defrost and I am done thinking about it until it has to get prepared.

Again, this system is to be tailor-made for you. If you shop every two weeks, work with a two-week meal plan. If you shop once a month, plan out a month-long meal plan. The idea is to get your menu planned *ahead* of time, not hours before you need it.

As far as breakfast and lunch are concerned, I have tried a variety of things. The one thing that I have found which makes them both much easier is to plan out what each day will be. I have found that it is easier for us to follow a plan for breakfast more so than with lunch.

Day	Breakfast	Lunch
Monday	Waffles	Sandwiches
Tuesday	Muffins and yogurt	Sandwiches
Wednesday	Cereal	Leftovers
Thursday	Oatmeal	Hot dogs
Friday	Cereal	Quesadillas
Saturday	Baked oatmeal	Leftovers
Sunday	Pancakes	Whatever ☺

We have tended to get away from the lunch schedule and I have noticed that lunches are more chaotic and take longer to eat and clean up. Most of us in our house feel that lunch is a necessary evil, so everyone just tries to find something that they think will be palatable. Unfortunately, this is not the most efficient way to do lunch for 8 people every day.

I have heard of other ways that people handle their meal issues. Some people like to cook a double recipe of a dinner and then freeze it for later use. Some people like to set aside one weekend a month and cook all kinds of different meals that they can freeze for later use. I know of others who shop in multiple stores, so they have a different list pre-made for each store. You could also try coming up with a couple of different weeks' worth of meals and then just rotating them. At one time, I had a list of our favorite recipes organized by the type of meat that was in them. I would use this list to help me quickly think of meals to plan for the week. I have a bunch of cookbooks and my goal is to one day go through all of them and write down which recipes in them I would like to try! In other words, there are many ways that you can try to organize your meals so that they are not a burden on your day. The important thing is that you should have some sort of plan in place.

The last thing I will mention in this section is snacks. I will admit that after having a few children, I got really tired of hearing "I'm hungry" all day long. In order to combat that problem, I instituted a 10:00 snack time and a 3:00 snack time. This way everyone knows that if you eat breakfast you can have a snack in a few hours to tide you over until lunch time. The same goes between lunch and dinner. This does work reasonably well and everyone knows what to expect.

As we discussed in the Chore chapter, everyone in our house has something to do when it comes to meal time. These chores are rotated on a monthly basis. My motto: get your kids involved in as many tasks as you can. Every-one benefits when you do that!

If you didn't assign meal and kitchen chores to your children while you were working on the Chore chapter, go back and do that before you move on.

Meal-Related Chores
Prepare meals—older girls and mom take turns
Set the table
Clear the table
Wash dishes
Dry dishes
Put dishes away
Wipe down counters and table
Sweep floor
Empty dishwasher
Load dishwasher

There isn't really much to do now in the way of planning out anything for this section. The next time you need to grocery shop, if you haven't done so already, make yourself a computerized grocery list. It really does help the list-making process and shopping go a lot faster. Also, start planning your dinners ahead of time. This is a must! If you take some time to set up your meal time system and plan out those dinners, it will save you huge amounts of time each and every day that can be better spent on something else.

Sample Grocery List

Bread: white   buns

Jelly

Coffee   Coffee filters

_____

Mustard   A-1   Mayo

Olives   BBQ sce   Pickles

Salad Dressing _____

Mexican _____

Oriental _____

Canned vegies _____

Tomato sce_____ Paste

Diced tomatoes _____

Noodles: most   spag

egg   cream.   lasagna

Spag Sce _____

Stuffing

Tuna

Soup _____

Rice: Brown   Wild

Pizza Sce

Juice: _____

Canned Fruit:_____

_____

Flour   Bkg pdwr   B. soda

Sugar: White   Brown

Powdered

Oil: Olive   Baking

spices: _____

Muffins

Cereal: _____

Oatmeal   Syrup

Toilet paper   Napkins

Kleenex   Paper towels

Paper plates

Tin foil   Lg. Baggies

Saran   Sand. Baggies

Garbage bags

Pop: _____

Butter: Salt   no salt

Yogurt   sour cream

eggs   milk   creamer

Lunchmeat: _____

_____

Cheese: Cheddar   mozz   mexican

Cream   Parmesan   feta

Taco shells   hot dogs

Chicken Breast _____   whole chicken

Ground Turkey   Turkey breast

Hamburger: _____

Pork chops _____

Other: _____

_____

Fruit: _____

_____

onion: green   white

carrots   celery   green pepper

Potatoes: white   red

cucumber   garlic   tomatoes

zucchini   lettuce

other: _____

_____

Frozen veggies: _____

Ravioli   Garlic bread

Dough

Frozen juice: OJ   apple

Ice cream   cool whip

Snacks: _____

Crackers: _____

Cookies

Toothpaste: us   kids

Deodorant   girls   boys

Hair spray   mousse   shampoo

Tylenol   decong.

Chapter Six
Husband, Family, and Personal Time

Now that we've tackled the biggest rocks for most people, we are going to cover the last couple at one time—your husband, your family, and yourself. These are the categories that should round out the rest of your daily schedule. I thought it would be easier to cover them all at one time because usually these are not areas that we assign very specific items to. More often than not, we just assign blocks of time to them. For example, from 7:00 till 8:00 is family time. This is usually sufficient for most people. You do not have to put down exactly what your family will be doing during this time if you do not want to.

Let us first consider our husbands. How easy it is to overlook that very important man at the head of the family. I have read some very good books on letting your husband be the head of your household, which I have included at the end of this workbook in case you are interested. There is so much that could be said about this subject, but suffice it to say that God has placed our husbands at the head of our family and we need to honor that God-given authority. Do we treat him that way? I know it was an eye-opener for me when I saw how much control I was taking away from my husband. I saw how much I had trained my children to look to me for direction and not to my husband. I also saw what an incredible difference it made in our household when I finally abdicated my place on the throne and gave it back to my husband (although I still find myself trying to overthrow the King every once in a while!).

So, with that in mind, how much of your day, right now, do you devote to your husband? If you already give him a lot of time and attention, then great; it will be easy to fill it right in. If your answer was closer to, "Time? Am I supposed to give him some of my time???" then you have some things to consider. Some people find that the best way for them to devote time to their husband is to set up a date night that they stick to once a week. It does not mean that you need to go anywhere. If your circumstances do not permit you to leave the house, then find other creative ways to devote a block of time at least one night a week to spending time with each other.

My husband and I found that this isn't what we like to do. We tried it for a while but then couldn't figure out what to do if date night came around and we didn't feel like doing anything together. Trying to reschedule never worked! What we prefer to do is to spend a little bit of time with each other every day. Some days he will call me on his way home from work, which allows us time to catch up on things. Other days we will spend time together after the kids go to bed and before one of us passes out. I'm not sure how we manage it some days, but we are able to communicate quite effectively this way every day and we enjoy spending this time together on a daily basis.

If you need improvement in this area, think about how you can set aside time in your day just for your husband. Again, maybe it won't be an hour a day, but make sure that you take at least some time out of your busy life every day and devote it to your husband.

One of the joys of homeschooling is that it gives us a lot of time to do things together as a family. Although some days you may be wondering if that is a good thing, most days I am sure you realize that it is. Is there a certain amount of time you want to schedule into your day for family time? Maybe it would include time to go for a walk together, pray together, read a book out loud, or watch a family movie. Whatever it is, if it is important for you to spend time together as a family, then you should schedule time into your day for it.

Last, but not least, what about your personal time??? After all, there are things that you need to get done that don't involve your children or your husband. Maybe you want to exercise. Maybe you want time to read a book. How about sewing or any other hobby you like to do? What about gardening or a personal apostolate? Maybe it is even something as mundane as being able to do your budgeting and pay your bills. Whatever it is, every mom needs some time every day to accomplish the things on her personal to do list.

So where do we find it? This is where the schedule comes in handy. You will never be able to put down on a schedule all of the minute details that make up your list of responsibilities. You can, however, block off time each day (or maybe every other day) when you know that everyone else will be reasonably occupied so that you can try to tackle some of those items.

Once you have your schedule in place, you will know that on most days, for example, you should be done with school by 3:00. You also know that on most days you don't have to start dinner until 4:30. That gives you 1 ½ hours to set aside some time to tackle your personal responsibilities. Three days a week you could exercise during that time. One other day could be used to pay bills. Another day, you could spend that time running errands or going on appointments. Again, it is not necessary to schedule specifics in to this time block, it is just important to *find* this block of time. Also, if you know that every day from 3:00–4:30 you will have some time to do the things you need to do, you are less likely to get sidetracked with them during what should be your prayer, chore, or school time.

I will be the first to admit, if there is a part of my schedule that I don't stick to, it is usually this part. Weeks may go by where this part of the day is up for grabs. The good thing, though, is that I know that my other bases are covered. I've got my prayer time locked in, school is pretty well set, and chores have their own time, so I don't feel too bad if the rest of the day or evening is up for grabs.

Before you begin working on this part of your day, let's stop and say a prayer.

Dear Lord, please help me to see the importance of setting aside time each day for my husband, for all of us to be together as a family, and for myself. Give me Your wisdom, Lord, so that I can see where it is in my day You want me to make time for these important areas. I know that every day can be different, but help me not to let too much time go by where I don't devote part of my day to the important people in my life. I love You and I thank You Lord for all that You have given me. Amen.

For this section, all you need to do is answer the questions listed on the next two pages and try to come up with some ideas for each of the three categories. When it comes time for the master schedule, you should have a good idea of how much time you want to devote to each of these three areas.

Husband Time

Do you think that you spend an adequate amount of time with your husband each day?

If no, how much time would you like to devote to your husband each day?

What time of the day would this occur?

For future reference, list some of the things that you would like to do with your husband during your time together.

Family Time

Is there any time every day that you would like to set aside for family time? If so, list those time(s).

For future reference, list some of the things you would like to do together during family time.

Personal Time

Outside of your prayer time, how much time do you think you need per day in order to get things done?

List the times that you think this is likely to occur.

Make a list of the tasks that you need to do (or want to do) that have not been covered thus far. Next to each item, mark whether this is to be done daily, weekly, or monthly.

Chapter 7
Putting It All Together

We have arrived at the moment you have all been waiting for. Now is the time to put all of this together into one grand schedule. If you have done all the work up until now, you can move forward. If you haven't done the work, stop now and do it! It will make much more sense if you have done all of your homework.

Remember this is not a do or die schedule. It is a guideline of how you would like each day to go, knowing in advance that it is not often that things will fall perfectly into place. I can't stress this enough. This is an outline for you to follow so that on good days your day runs smoothly and on bad days you can regroup and jump back in wherever you should be.

Maybe one last example would help. Imagine that tomorrow you wake up on time, pray, and your day gets off to a good start, but then your husband calls and says that he has locked his keys in his car and he needs you to run out and bring him the extra set. By the time you pack up the kids, get him his keys, and return home, it is 10:00 and half your morning is gone. Instead of flipping out and doing nothing because you feel like the day is already ruined, you can look to your schedule and do one of two things: Replace what is left of the morning with some of the things you missed or just start where you should be at 10:00 and make up the things you missed during free time or during the next day. Don't get bogged down by the schedule or thrown off course by unexpected events! Use the schedule as the tool it is meant to be.

This is a big moment, so take a moment to pray before you begin:

> *Lord, this is it: the time when I try to organize all of the inspirations You have given me thus far. Please send the Holy Spirit to help me to know how my plan should fall into place. I ask that You make it easy for me to put this all together and then give me the grace to implement it into my life. I thank You, Lord, for everything. Amen.*

So where do you start? Here is a list of all of the completed worksheets that you need to have in front of you right now:

1. Prayer Worksheet
2. Chore Worksheet 2
3. School Worksheets 2 and 3
4. Husband, Family, and Personal Worksheets.

I think it will be helpful to have the sample Master Schedule sheets in front of you so that you can follow along as you read through what you will be doing. These sheets can be found at the end of this chapter.

Finally, you will need the blank Master Schedule sheets, also found at the end of this chapter. I would recommend photocopying them so that you can use them multiple times. If you have more than 5 kids, just make sure to copy another set of blank sheets and put the rest of the children in on the next set of sheets.

To help you assemble the Master Schedule, I have included a list of the steps you will need to take and the order you will do them in.

How to fill in the Master Schedule

1. Write the names of your children in the boxes at the top of the blank Master Schedule. Again, just refer to the sample Master Schedule if you are unsure of what it is you are supposed to do.

2. Decide what time your school day is going to begin and then put a mark in the box with that time. If your day will begin with Mass, then put a mark in the box when Mass will begin. If you go to daily Mass at the same time every day, then that is the starting time that you will be dealing with instead of a school starting time.

3. Next, you need to decide what time your kids will get up so that they can eat breakfast, do their morning chores, and be ready to start school or leave for Mass. The sample schedule is made with the assumption that we are not leaving the house the first thing in the morning.

4. Next you have to decide how much time *you* need in order to be ready to meet the children when they get up. This will be based on the morning prayers that you have decided you want to say and how much time it takes you to get showered/dressed/cleaned up, bed made, coffee, or whatever.

   I know that I need 30 minutes for prayer in the morning and 30 minutes to shower/dress and make my bed. Therefore, I get up at 6:00 because I will wake my children at 7:00.

5. Go ahead and fill in your schedule up till the point of finishing breakfast and being ready to start school or leave the house. Remember, this is not a schedule about how you are doing things now *unless* you are perfectly happy with the way your mornings go. If you have a workable morning schedule, then it will be easy to fill in this part of the chart. If you want more discipline to your morning because there are things that you would like to accomplish but can't (perhaps because you never know what time you or your kids are going to get up), then take some time to plan something that will accomplish what you want but still be workable for your family.

6. Okay, the next step is an easy one. Decide what time you and your family will take your lunch break so that you can eat, and do any mid-day

prayers or chores that you have assigned. Mark that time block on your schedule.

7. Now, to the best of your ability, fill in your school schedule. Make sure as you do this that you do not schedule yourself or anyone else to be in two different places at the same time. Use your school time planning worksheets to help you out. I usually start by blocking off any times that we will all be together, then move to any times that I need to work with individuals, then move to the times when each child is working on their own or with other children.

You might not get this whole part of the schedule filled in today. Or you may fill it in and then tomorrow, after you have had time to ponder it, you may decide to move some things around. That's okay. Work with the schedule until it flows smoothly. You may find that you even need to change it in a few months as your school year progresses. Your schedule is your tool and it should be flexible enough to fit your needs.

8. The next block you are going to fill in is your dinner time. Block off the time when your family will more than likely be sitting down to dinner. Hopefully it is about the same time every night.

9. Now you know how much time you have between the end of school and the dinner hour. This is where you will fill in items for you and your children from your personal list or your family list. You may decide to fill this time with running errands or scheduling lessons. Whatever it is, fill in this time with whatever you think your family will be doing. Don't forget to leave time for dinner preparation. If there is nothing specific that you will be doing every day at the same time, feel free to block it off as free time.

10. After dinner comes dinner clean-up, so write that time on your schedule *now*. Remember, it is far better to take the time immediately after dinner to clean up your kitchen than it is to leave it sit and think you will get back to it later. In my mind, there is nothing that will start my day off worse than walking into a kitchen full of last night's dishes.

11. The next time to fill in is bed time for all of your children and then yourself. You cannot get up on time in the morning if you never have a set bed time. Make it easy on yourself and stick to your bed time as much as

possible. Don't forget to end your day with the prayer routine you set up on your prayer worksheet.

12. The time between the end of dinner chores and bed time is now yours to fill in. Unless you have something specific you will do every evening, such as read aloud or rosary, you can probably just fill in the evenings with Family Time. You only need to be as specific as you want to be.

13. Don't forget to put some time in your schedule for your husband. Whether it is in the morning before work or in the evening before bed, it is important to set some time aside to connect with each other.

Can you believe that is it? You now have a plan that will help you to be more organized. Not only that, it will bring a sense of peace because you know that all the important things that are necessary for having a smoothly run household are built into your day. Now all you have to do is follow it.

If you really want this schedule to be your friend, to work for you, and for your life to be more stress-free, I believe there are some crucial elements that you must embrace.

You must:

Wake up on time
Be faithful to your prayer plan—morning, noon, and night
Stick to getting your basic chores done every day
Be flexible when God steps in and alters your plan
Look back to your schedule to regain control of your day if you lose it
Spend time with your husband
Go to bed on time

A mother who has a plan that she follows is more likely to be:

Prayerful
Rested
Charitable
Joyful
Able to spread that joy to others
Able to effectively handle activities or apostolate work outside the home
Able to more effectively accomplish God's will for her life

I know you can do it! Our God is a God of order, and He loves to see faithful subjects trying diligently to order their own lives and homes so that they can more effectively do His will. May God bless you as you venture forth on your newly organized life.

Sample Master Schedule

Time	Mom	Megan	Teresa	Rebecca	Timmy	Mary
5:30 am						
6:00	Get up, prayers					
6:30	Get ready	Get up	Get up			
7:00	Rest of kids up, breakfast ready, eat, breakfast chores, kids get ready					
7:30						
8:00	Travel and Mass					
8:30						
9:00	With Anthony	Biology	Botany	French	Typing	Grammar
9:30	With Mary	French	Religion	Religion	Religion	Math w/ Mary
10:00	With Timmy, Rebecca	Am. Govt	French	Math w/ Mom	Math w/ Mom	Spelling
10:30	With Meg, Teresa	Math w/ mom	Math w/ mom	Grammar/ Spelling	Grammar/ Spelling	Handwriting
11:00	Unit Study Time/ Geography Time					
11:30						
12:00 pm	Lunch—eat, lunch chores, free time					
12:30						
1:00	Be available to help kids with schoolwork	Am History/ Literature	Am History/ Literature	Read w/ Mary	French	Read w/ Rebecca
1:30		Apologetics	Piano w/ Timmy	Beautiful Girlhood	Piano w/ Teresa	Play w/ Anthony
2:00		Website	Silent Reading			
2:30		Website	Free Time			

Sample Master Schedule

Time	Mom	Megan	Teresa	Rebecca	Timmy	Mary
3:00	Appts, phone calls, bills, work	Free Time				
3:30						
4:00						
4:30	Dinner Prep			Pick up assigned rooms		
5:00		Pre-dinner chores				
5:30	Dinner Time					
6:00	With Hubby	Post dinner chores				
6:30						
7:00	Family Rosary					
7:30	Family Time or Free Time					
8:00						
8:30	Finish day's work, computer time	Free Time			Bed Time	
9:00		Free Time		Bed Time		
9:30		Bed Time				
10:00	Prayers					
10:30	Bed Time					
11:00						
11:30						
12:00 am						

Sample Master Schedule

Time	Anthony				
5:30 am					
6:00					
6:30					
7:00	Get up, ready, eat				
7:30	Finish getting ready				
8:00	Mass				
8:30					
9:00	Reading, Math W/ Mom				
9:30	Hand-writing				
10:00	Spelling				
10:30	Grammar				
11:00	Unit Study Time				
11:30					
12:00 pm	Lunch				
12:30	Lunch				
1:00	Free Time				
1:30					
2:00					
2:30					

Sample Master Schedule

Time	Anthony				
3:00	Free Time				
3:30	Free Time				
4:00	Free Time				
4:30	Pick up assigned rm				
5:00	Set table				
5:30	Dinner				
6:00	Free time				
6:30	Free time				
7:00	Rosary				
7:30	Family Time, Free Time				
8:00	Family Time, Free Time				
8:30	Bed Time				
9:00					
9:30					
10:00					
10:30					
11:00					
11:30					
12:00 am					

Master Schedule

Time					
5:30 a.m.					
6:00					
6:30					
7:00					
7:30					
8:00					
8:30					
9:00					
9:30					
10:00					
10:30					
11:00					
11:30					
12:00 p.m					
12:30					
1:00					
1:30					
2:00					

Time						
2:30						
3:00						
3:30						
4:00						
4:30						
5:00						
5:30						
6:00						
6:30						
7:00						
7:30						
8:00						
8:30						
9:00						
9:30						
10:00						
10:30						
11:00						
11:30						
12:00 am						

Afterword

It has been six years since I put this book together and my, a lot has happened in that time. My children are all older, for one thing. I have graduated three from homeschool high school with two in high school right now and the last two in grade school. My life is different and much more hectic, if you can believe that, than when I first wrote this all down.

I thought it was important to tell you about this because I am now on the other side of toddlers and babies and schooling seven children at one time. I've been through the trenches and have come out, or at least am working on coming out, on the other side. You need to know how it turns out, don't you?

First off, let me just tell you that having older children and young adults in the house is a whole other ball game. Having a lot of small children is hard, but at least you can tell them where to be and when to be there. Trying to manage a household with people who have their own schedules and their own ideas on how things should go brings managing my home to a whole different level. I cannot imagine how much more chaotic it would be if I had not invested the time in organizing things when they were littler.

I have to say that all of the years of teaching them to schedule things and be organized have paid off. I see them doing it in their own lives now. Throughout college, work, and the myriad of activities they've been in, they've learned that making lists and planning things out is what makes it all doable. When stress levels get high, they sit down and analyze what needs to be done, when it needs to be finished, and how long it is going to take, and then make lists and start tackling them. I can say that there is still a rhythm to our day-to-day lives, even though a lot has changed, and even though the front door has been replaced with a revolving one.

There was another, unexpected positive outcome to all of this scheduling. In January of 2016, our youngest son, who was 10 at the time, was diagnosed as a Type 1 Diabetic. Talk about throwing your family life into the middle of a big heap of stress and chaos! But as I sat there that first day listening to the dietician telling us about some of the best ways to help him, I realized that we were already doing those things!

Regular meal times—✓

Regular snack times—✓

Regular bed time—✓

Not a lot of fast/processed foods—✓

I realized what a huge help it was to already have him in a routine, eating good meals, and getting a good amount of sleep. If we had had to change our entire lifestyle on top of figuring this whole diabetic thing out, I can tell you that it would have been way more stressful than it already was.

My point is that you never know what is coming around the next bend. It may be something good or it may be something bad. Either way, it could be something that might make you thankful that you took the time right now to organize your day and put some routinization into your life and the lives of your children.

Endnotes

1. Francis Fernandez, *In Conversation with God: Meditations for each day of the year*, vol. 2 (London: Scepter, 1997), 203.
2. Fernandez, 304.
3. Fernandez, vol. 4, 297-299.
4. Fernandez, 300.
5. Father John Harden, *Father Hardon's Catholic Prayer Book with Meditations*, (Kentucky: Eternal Life, 1999), p. 268.

Resources

This is a list of resources that I have found very helpful over the years:

In Conversation with God, Meditations for each day of the year by Francis Fernandez—7 volume set

Abandonment to Divine Providence by Jean-Pierre De Caussade

Trustful Surrender to Divine Providence by St. Claude de la Columbiere and Fr. Jean Baptiste Saint-Jure

Created to be His Help Meet by Debi Pearl available from No Greater Joy Ministries at www.nogreaterjoy.org—this is a Protestant publication

The Spiritual Exercises of St. Ignatius—a silent retreat presented by the priests of Miles Christi www.mileschristi.org

16301019R00038

Printed in Great Britain
by Amazon